DAVID JAMES
SHE DANCES LIKE MUSSOLINI

Copyright © 2009
David James
March Street Press
3413 Wilshire
Greensboro NC 27408
marchstreetpress.com
rbixby@earthlink.net
isbn 1-59661-105-7

Atlanta Review: One Gag to Go
Brix: Probation After Death
Caliban: The Politics of an Idiot, The Music of an Idiot
California Quarterly: The Season for Leaving
Chattahoochee Review: Dear Hairline
Chiron Review: Dear Future
Driftwood Review: Dear Feet
Feh: The Romantic
Fugue: How to Fall in Love With Country Music
Goodfoot: The Art of Practice
Iowa Review: The Tired of Your Present Life Tree Game, The Moo Game
Jam To-day: Dead Horses
Lake Effect: Return of the Grim Reaper
Literary Review: The Vision of an Idiot
Lucid Moon: For Open Mike Readers
Mid-Atlantic Review: The Evolution of a Pregnant Woman
New Mexico Literary Review: The Plain Truth
New York Quarterly: View of a Pair
Penny Dreadful: Only on Sundays
Poetry East: A Heaven Chair
Puerto Del Sol: Only So Much No
Quarterly West: If Men Ran the World
Rattle: How to Make Amends
Sierra Madre Review: She Dances Like Mussolini, Eating Trees
Slant: Dear Memory, Instructions for My Funeral
South Coast Poetry Journal: The Meaning of Life
Steam Ticket: I'll Take Your Face
Thundersandwich: The Last Thing a Man Would Ever Say

    I thank the Michigan Council for the Arts for a grant during which time some of these poems were written. I thank Michael Mink for the inspiration of the title poem. And I thank March Street Press for publishing three chapbooks, *I Dance Back, I Will Peel This Mask Off,* and *Trembling in Someone's Palm,* in which many of these poems first appeared.

She Dances Like Mussolini • 5
The Politics of an Idiot • 6
Eating Trees • 7
One Gag to Go • 8
Dear Feet • 10
The Art of Practice • 11
How to Make Amends • 12
Dear Memory • 13
If Men Ran the World • 14
A Poet's Life: Take Two • 15
Instructions on How to Fall in Love • 16
The Music of an Idiot • 17
The Hangover of Love • 18
For Open Mike Readers • 19
A Heaven Chair • 20
Probation After Death • 21
Trash Talk for Sigmund Freud • 22
Hands and Tongues • 24
The Evolution of a Pregnant Woman • 25
The New Life Soup Game • 26
Dear Hairline • 27
Only So Much No • 28
Dead Horses • 29
I Do Whatever My Rice Krispies Tell Me To • 30
Dear Penis • 31
The Vision of an Idiot • 33
The Romantic • 34
My Edson Phase • 35
View of a Pair • 36
Only on Sundays • 37
The Other Side of the Coin • 38
Dear Future • 39
The Tired of Your Present Life Tree Game • 40
The Poet: Number Two • 41
Voices • 42
Dear Death • 43
The Meaning of Life • 44
Instructions for My Funeral • 45

How Do You Spell Relief? • 47
The Pretend You're Not Alive Game • 48
One Night Stand • 49
The Moo Game • 50
The Season for Leaving • 51
The Substitute • 52
God Takes Up Golf • 53
The Plain Truth • 54
Last Thing a Man Would Ever Say • 56
How to Fall in Love With Country Music • 57
A Burning Bush of Sorts • 58
Return of the Grim Reaper • 59
I'll Take Your Face • 60

For Debbie, Collin, Nathan, Leah, Yasuko and Cloud...
May nothing ever hold you back.

"Thoughts are free and subject to no rule. On them rests the freedom of humanity, and they tower above the light of nature."
—Paracelsus

"The most powerful prayer and ultimately the most powerful to obtain all things, and the worthiest work of all, is what proceeds from a free mind. A free mind has power to perform all things."
—Meister Eckhart

She Dances Like Mussolini

Short & stout,
her hair unable to fly loose
        from her head,
my blind date marches across
        the dance floor,
arms jerking, her
 whole body banging
into others.
With each impact, she salutes
        & shouts up into the music.
This is the last time, I tell myself,
the last time.
But in minutes, she has everyone in the bar
marching in rows, everyone ordering Chianti.
        Bodies barge and ram, people scream
& kick their legs out in time to the beat.
        I can't understand a word of the shouting,
the gutteral, grunting phrases.
        My date winks at me across the length of the floor
& then starts this way, dancing like Mussolini.
        & God knows I'm sick:
        I dance back.

The Politics of an Idiot

If a politician has dark eyebrows, his signature is illegible. His wife has affairs. His children sleep in their underwear only. And he will not tell you the whole truth.

If a politician has light eyebrows, he owns a bird, but forgets to feed it. He drives a red car. His house has three entrances, seven exits. His lawn is sprayed with chemicals. And he will cost you.

If a politician has large, bushy eyebrows, he once worked in a clothing store and was fired for insubordination. He doesn't know the names of all of his cousins. His golf swing is unorthodox. And he will turn against you the minute he assumes office.

If a politician has no eyebrows, elect him. He is the one who has nothing to hide.

Eating Trees

I'd like
to eat a tree
just grab one of these cedars
my grandpa drove here from Detroit
forty-five years ago
to plant near Lake Huron
two stories tall now
just grab one in my hand
and devour it in large bites
branches   leaves   bark
flying out of my mouth
as I chew through nests
old kite strings   a lost glider
swallowing the initials
my father carved into it
before I was alive
I want to eat so many trees
and keep them inside me
to have more of this world
than I can now
than I'll ever be able to
I'd like to eat
every great day like a cedar
all the wondrous people and laughs
the faces and bodies and voices
the hugs and bonfires
and drinks and leaps
eating tree after tree after tree
I want to die
by explosion
refusing to shit any of it out

One Gag to Go
"In the end, everything is a gag."
—Charlie Chaplin

1.
My grandpa,
dying in the hospital,
used his plastic fake puke daily
on the floor, the table,
a gag that never failed
until his own heart did.

2.
A woman walks into a pharmacy,
asks for poison to kill her husband.
The pharmacist says, "Ma'am, I'm sorry,
but I can't give that to you."
The woman hands over a photo
of her husband in bed
with the pharmacist's wife.
"Oh, you didn't tell me you
had a prescription."

3.
I'm not afraid of death.
I'm not afraid of death.
I'm not afraid of death.
As Woody Allen once said,
"I'm not afraid to die.
I just don't want to be there
when it happens."

4.
The little boy sat
on his grandfather's lap.
The boy said, "Grandpa,
will you make the sound of a frog?"

"No. That's silly."
"Please," the boy said,
"make a sound like a frog."
"Now why do you want me to do that?"
the grandpa asked.
"Because Daddy said when you croak,
we're going to Disneyworld."

5.
I want to die
laughing. In the middle
of a belly laugh, crying
from too much joy,
bent over and exhausted,
let the big one come
and wrestle me to the ground:
one final gag and I'm
gone.

Dear Feet

Nothing stands between us.
You two are my Indian scouts,
Surveying the territory, sent out
Ahead to carve the trail,
Blaze a path,
Start the fire, and I am
At your mercy.
If you go left, I go left.
If you climb, I follow.
When you run, I am dragged behind
Like excess baggage.

If I've taken you for granted
Over the years, forgive me.
So far from the head, you live a life
Blinded most of the time
By cotton and nylon, ushered into shoes,
Tied, bound, sweaty and captured.
You dream each night of being free
From me, jogging alone through the open fields,
Climbing mountains, jumping into streams.
You imagine heading out on your own,
Naked and fleshy, joining in
The company of others, whole packs
Of wild feet living in the woods,
Huddled toe-to-toe to keep warm
Through the cold nights.

Instead, you're stuck here
To me, treading along that fine line,
Like the rest of us,
Between despair
And duty.

The Art of Practice

She kissed him hard, laid him down, sat on top and unbuttoned his shirt. Kissed his breast, his stomach. Kissed his neck, ear, forehead. She squeezed a lemon on his chest, rubbed it into his skin, tongued off the sweet-sour juice.

If she ever found someone to love, she would know what to do.

How to Make Amends

He was hungry, so he ate the couch, the one with the pull-out bed. Of course, when the wife came home, she was disgusted.

"Now what will we sit on, asshole? Last week it was the coffee table, the week before, two kitchen chairs and a lamp. What next, the bed?"

He hadn't thought of eating the bed, but the idea was appealing. It probably would taste like sleep. Comfort food. He couldn't respond to her—she was always right, so he went upstairs to lie down. Somehow, the bed knew what was coming. It shivered in fear. The man stroked the mattress, saying, "Don't worry. I won't eat you. I promise." As the bed settled down, the man fell asleep and dreamed of eating the bed, mattress, baseboard, springs, pillows. He stuffed everything in his mouth, chewing, crunching, swallowing until he could no longer stand up. He laid there on the floor in the bedroom. When his wife came home after work, she undressed, climbed on top of him, slid under some loose sheets and slept. His chest rose and fell in time to her steady breathing. Wrapping himself around her, he knew she would be next. He would eat her and finally there would be peace between them, which was all he ever really wanted.

Dear Memory

I've missed you.
At least, I think I have.
I've forgotten when you were last with me;
You've walked out so many times.
And where to? A six-month poker game
With my cerebellum?
A drinking binge with the subconscious?
It's crazy here without you—
Who are all these people?
And where did I leave my car keys?
Was I supposed to pick up some milk?
Not a day goes by without a curse
Thrown in your direction, wherever that is.
You could write at least,
Or call once in awhile,
Let me know you're alive, well,
Lost perhaps, but planning to head back.
I hear nothing. You've left me
To stew in my own broth,
Trying to keep my name straight.
The kids barely seem to tolerate
This lump of man wandering in their house.
The woman who sleeps with me
Shakes her head a lot, pats my hand.
I leave for work each morning,
But hell if I know where to go.
I drive and drive and try to think.
Because of you, or the lack of you,
I'd end it all right now
If I could remember how.

If Men Ran the World

"When your girlfriend needed to talk to you during the game, she'd appear in a little box in the corner of the TV screen during a time-out."

& the TV announcer's blathering drone
would dim slowly
as your girlfriend's voice
gets louder, & better,
thanks to enhanced audio technology.
She comes across as ultra-sexy,
a temptress turned on
by your uncanny ability to sit for hours
in front of football games & drink beer.
She asks if you need another refill
in a tone that moves something
below your waist.
She poses on screen, mouthing kisses
to you, showing ample cleavage.
You click the food button
& your girl times it so the bratwurst & beans
are served at half-time or during
redundant post-game commentary.
As she leaves, she dances the seductive dance
of love.

The fact is if men really ran the world,
virtually all interaction with women
would be like this—one click
& she's in a little box in the corner of the TV,
another click, she brings in ribs & beer,
click, she's naked,
click, click, she's gone.

A Poet's Life: Take Two

If this was a movie,
I'd be taller, with hair,
with beautiful teeth.
The women would lust after me
and would be willing to die
for one passionate kiss
from these gorgeous lips.
The action music would start
as my archrival poet barges into the room,
and challenges me, mano y mano.
I land a right hook and send him sailing
over the first three rows; he stands up
and tackles me like a little boy.
I throw him off, grab a chair
and break it over his head,
the least vulnerable part of his anatomy.
He pulls a gun and fires while I catch
the bullets, one, two, three, between my teeth
and spit them out like watermelon seeds.
I walk over and, right to his face,
say, "Your poems make me sick."
Then, with one quick slap, I render him unconscious.
At this point, a messenger arrives with a telegram
informing me that I have just won
the Pulitzer, the Nobel Peace Prize, a Purple Heart.
The audience would hoist me above their heads,
and there would be a joyful celebration that spreads
throughout the city in my name, in my honor.
If this was a movie, I'd be offered a zillion dollars
to write my next poem, which I would reluctantly accept,
and the most beautiful woman in the universe
would take my arm, promise to type my poems
and love me unconditionally.

The movie would end as I wink at the camera
and say, fading into the sunset,
        "A poet's life
          is really cool."

Instructions on How to Fall in Love

Collect the scales
from two northern Michigan walleye,
capture a June bug in May,
pick out ten fossils of different colors
and mix them all with birch bark,
bee wings, rose petals, wild ferns,
and the chopped up feathers
from a mourning dove.
Pour this potion
at your doorstep and wait.
Nothing will happen,
but it will keep you busy for awhile.
The real trick is to stop caring
about love or romance or attraction.
Close your eyes and turn your brain back
to the year before you ever held hands,
or wanted to. Stop looking
for Mr. or Mrs. Right and accept
everything at face value:
instead of reading into the eyes,
say blue, brown, hazel.
Instead of imagining a touch on the shoulder
meant something, say arm, hand, finger.
Say cheek, lips, mouth.
Say laugh, wrestle, hug.
Think anything but love
and do everything but think.
The way to fall in love
is to trip yourself,
surprised that you never saw it
in front of you, or beside you,
or reading to you,
or banging its head on your chest
saying, It's me, it's me,
it's really me.

The Music of an Idiot

He doesn't own a radio or cassette, tape deck or CD player. The closest thing to a musical instrument in his apartment is the one metal spoon, which he saves for special meals. His music is the world's, though in a million attempts he could never think of it that way.

The sound of sparrows in the eaves trough, early morning, picking out bugs, seeds.

The dripping of rain after a heavy downpour.

Snoring from a vagrant on a park bench.

A curtain brushing on the window in the wind.

Sneezes, farts, yawns, coughs.

His goldfish leaping up out of the water.

A dog, two blocks over, barking.

Any train whistle, any time of day.

When he is near real music, it confuses him. It grates against his thick brain, scraping like cheese or lettuce, the notes dropping in thin pieces on the ground. He carefully steps away to find a pond where some ducks are flapping their wings, where frogs are calling him by his secret name.

The Hangover of Love

"If I Could Love Like I Can Drink,
I'd Be Barfing Up Kisses All Night."
—Imaginary song title, JOHNNY CARSON

Your love is like a horse:
men stick to you like glue.
Just say the word
and I'm yours tonight.
My old lady left me
chewing my hide raw,
so I need someone to love
before my money runs out.
Let's you and me
get on the saddle together
and ride on up to the pearly gates.
God knows we deserve it
for living in this damn country.
Two more shots of Jack Daniels
and I'll be sick for your love.
A third and you'll be gorgeous.
I can feel my heart upchuck
to the sweet smell of manure
on your boots.
Let me brand you with the horn of plenty.
Let me plow through your wide fields
of desire.
What do you have to lose?
I got me a pick up, ten acres,
four pigs, and a John Deere.
Just say the word
and I'll throw up
everything for you.
My love is like a good bottle
of whiskey:
grab me anywhere
and I'll come.

If drinks were wishes
and drunks were hard candy,
you'd of been mine long ago,
sucking your way
into my heart.

For Open Mike Readers
an elitist poem

Don't think of yourself
as neophytes,
say rather you're
"poetically challenged"
and deserve this mike
as much as anybody.
The law is on your side.
And what do those featured writers
have over you other than
talent, publication, experience?
In every other way, you're equal.
She breathes, you breathe.
She eats, you eat.
She farts, you fart.
So come on up, proud and confident,
and read your poem about
the flowers in the meadow,
where you rhyme "in ya" with "zinnia,"
or the one about the beast inside,
gorging itself on the warm blood
of innocent mothers yet unborn.
Grab the mike, it's open,
and take your stand,
your three poems or five minutes,
whichever comes first.
You have every right in the world
to be here.

And we have every right
to leave.

A Heaven Chair

It was the chair to heaven. If you sat in it, and if it was your time to go, the chair rose up above the cathedral pillars, through the ceiling fresco, into the sky, catapulting you faster than the naked eye could see. In seconds, you found yourself standing up on a blue cloud, the chair descending back to earth for the next contestant. It was like a game show, people lining up for miles to take a turn on the heaven chair. The church did away with bingo night because of the new profits at $10 per sitting.

Even those who paid, sat, and had nothing happen were celebrities of a kind. Was this an omen that hell was in their future? Were they to be feared? Were they to be pitied? Or was it just not their time—come back in 10 or 20 years and see what happens?

I'll always remember my grandma. She sat down and the chair shot up through the roof. To this day, I can hear her frail voice screaming. I can't tell whether she's overjoyed or shitting her pants.

Probation After Death
the title of a sermon in Flint, Michigan

You never were lucky.
It was in the stars,
settling in the tea leaves,
certainly in your palms,
this knack for finding trouble:
flat tires, lost checks,
train accidents, premature balding.
Even as a kid, you were the only one
who hit liners through Bladecki's window,
the one caught stealing tomatoes
out of Mr. Jump's backyard.
If the police were going to randomly stop
anyone on the road, it'd be you,
with wine bottles on the floor,
your driver's license expired,
five parking tickets overdue.
But now you've gone and made
your biggest mistake, you died,
and you end up on probation.

Maybe God is waiting to see
how well you take to those new wings,
or how long you can stay afloat on a cloud.
Maybe He needs a tenor for the choir.
Probation might just be standard policy
for anyone heading up from Flint, Michigan.

But one Sunday morning,
in a lazy moment, slouched back against the pearly gates,
you'll forget where you are and say, "God dammit,"
and you'll be history,
waking up in someone's body,
in a town you've never heard of,
with yet another
life sentence.

Trash Talk for Sigmund Freud

"I have found little that is good about human beings.
In my experience, most of them are trash."
—SIGMUND FREUD

Are you talking trash
as in used tissues and candy wrappers,
or trash as in molded cottage cheese
and excrement?
It's no surprise,
given this inclination,
that your theories describe us
with pent-up aggression,
base animal instincts,
a preoccupation with our penises,
or the lack of them.
Your idea that we boys actually desire
to make love to our mothers
makes sense now.
Your whole life you were seeking
these aberrations, these abnormalities,
simply to prove your point.

Well, Siggy, no one believes you.
Your bizarre patients told you
what you wanted to hear:
the rest you made up to fit.
On some level,
you wanted to screw us all.
Your ego wasn't super;
it was a damp, frightened little creature.
You must have hit your head

as a child because only a Freudian slip
could explain your absurd motives.

Listen,
sometimes people do things
because they want to,
not for sex, not for power,
not for instinctual urges
they only dream about.
Here's some real trash talk:
Go back to the beginning,
                Sigmund,
                          and try again.

Hands and Tongues

Vanna walked up to the mirror and kissed her reflection. Then, she brought her right hand up and kissed it, a long and passionate kiss with no tongue. She hated tongues. They were like live sunburned clams to her.

Her hand came up to her face, eye-level, and spoke, "So, why don't we ever French kiss?"

"You know why."

"No, I don't. I'd like a little tongue sometimes."

Vanna looked disgusted. "I don't want this to get out of hand."

"As if it could," the hand said. "I'm a hand, dammit. I have no legs, no torso, no penis, no vagina. I'm a frigging hand."

"I don't trust myself," Vanna replied and shoved her hand beneath a throw pillow. It struggled to get out, but couldn't, and finally fell asleep. Vanna sighed. The tingling hurt a bit, miniature needles sticking in her palm and fingers, but it was better this way. The hand knew how to get under her skin. It was best to let the hand sleep and dream of other hands with large slimy tongues.

The Evolution of a Pregnant Woman

A man with perfectly normal genetic organization walks over to turn off the light. But as he flicks the switch with his index finger, a needle of electricity threads up his arm, weaving his body with wattage. At first he doesn't notice the illumination and climbs under the sheets into bed. When he closes his eyes, all he can see is white light arcing from his brain.

The man, now realizing other ways to save money, persuades his wife to be a gas oven. The children are ordered into becoming cans of vegetables, stacked neatly on the shelves. The grandmother of the family volunteers to be a young woman living a lonely, quiet life in the house.

Some evenings through the windows, you can see a man hanging from the ceiling, a quivering filament. A young woman opens the oven door like a womb and shoves a casserole inside. She leaves the kitchen and lies down on the couch, patting her slightly enlarged stomach. Fine strings of pain trail up into her body where at the end, she hopes, her many children cover the sky like kites.

The New Life Soup Game

Collect your dirty socks
for two weeks straight
and place them in a large pan
with chicken broth.
Season at will—
garlic, basil, onion,
cayenne pepper.
On those occasions
when you feel especially saucy,
use Red Hot or chili powder.
Simmer for three hours,
eleven minutes, and twenty-two seconds.
With scissors or lawn clippers,
cut the socks into thin slices,
noodle-like, and stir them back in
with chopped up pieces of yesterday's
newspaper and the hair of the dog
that last bit you.
Serve it up in plastic bowls
to eat only with plastic spoons
within ten miles of a plastic plant,
for best results.
Take very small sips,
and chew steadily for a long, long time.
After you've finished all the soup,
put your foot in your mouth
and swallow it.
Things will never
be the same
after that.

Dear Hairline

Where the hell are you going?
You're losing your grip with age,
falling up and back over my skull.
You seem to take pleasure
in undressing my forehead,
tossing precious hair
down the drain,
on the bathroom counter,
clumps sleeping on my pillow.
It won't be long now —
you'll keep slipping away
until you're alive only
in photographs and memories.
And I'll be a cue ball,
glaring into the future,
baldly going where bald men
have gone before.
I'll save money on barbers.
I'll buy a convertible.
I'll have a great hat collection.
I'll let me wife stroke my smooth skin,
buff my head with bee's wax.
The only hairline I'll have in five years
will be something I can hang out
on the clothesline, easy on,
easy off.

But who cares anyway?
Hairlines are for babies
and snotty-nosed boys.
Real men like us don't have to cover up
who we really are: with only our shine
and brains to get us through,
we accept what God
meant for us and head out
into the world,
face first.

Only So Much No

Forgive me,
but I won't take no for an answer.
It's time to stand up and refuse
the hundreds of rejection slips,
to kill any editor who says,
"Not this time, but try us again."
Any creative death will do
for the staff of the next magazine
to reply: "We liked these a lot,
but none seemed quite right for us."
Line them up and fire. Bomb them.
Scalp them and feed their hair
to the closest mailbox.
Let even the mail carriers
sweat a bit.
They're guilty by proxy.
Have the blow darts aimed
as they walk up to the door
with letters in hand.

There's only so much no
a person can take, and I'm there.
I pity the next editor who spits on my poems —
my return envelope has cyanide
sprinkled across the glue.
And they say I'm licked, hah!
I'll track them down
from university to university —
plastic explosives in their office doors,
brakes disconnected in the lots.

Soon, my poems will appear everywhere,
in all magazines, with feature stories,
centerfolds, my menacing face on the covers.
A creative frenzy, they'll say.
A mad genius to be reckoned with.
Before long, every editor in the world
will accept my poems sight unseen,
write me long personal letters,
invite me to her summer cottage on the Cape.
Of course, it would be a crime not to.

Dead Horses

"There's just nothing
like a dead horse."
—COLLIN, age 3

They are much easier
to mount this way.
Mother has nothing to fear
as Susie heads out to ride
the dead horse.
In fact, she saves hundreds
on grain, hay, veterinarian bills.
And yet the horse can still be groomed,
combed, brushed, prepared for show,
braids and ribbons displayed.
The two commands that always work
"Lay down. Play dead."

There's just nothing like a dead horse.
Easy to convert into a coffee table,
a bench chair, a conversation piece.
"So, how long have you had
your dead horse?" or
"Let's go back to my place
and I'll show you my dead horse."

A dead horse is quiet,
serene, majestic in an odd way,
requiring a minimum of care.
It's natural enough:
horses die, like everything,
but they aren't like everything.
So much power, so much pure grace.
It seems more of a disgrace
to bring the tractor in,
drag the body out to some meadow,
spend half the day digging.
So I pull it in the house,
this symbol of young America,
a perfect addition
to anyone's three bedroom ranch.

I Do Whatever
My Rice Krispies Tell Me To
(a bumper sticker)

you either believe or not:
the signs are everywhere

on the radio/in the pubic hairs along the sink
a bluejay at the feeder
the small eyes of a gas station clerk

the trick is to watch for them
listen to them
understand them

I lost the lottery once
after ignoring two license plates on I-75

I missed a job offer in Toledo
by not cleaning my car—as I look back,
the signs in the sunrise were obvious

a golden thread, invisible to us humans,
weaves from person to tree to event
to house to memory to tomorrow
it wants to be found/touched
it wants to lead us

from this certain disaster
to some kind of love
or holiness
maybe this poem is a sign/a message
maybe you
are the answer

Dear Penis

So, how are you doing
down there?
I hope things
are looking up,
for both of our sakes.
Like an albino mole,
you've lived your whole life
burrowed in dark, cramped corners.
Once, when I was much younger,
I laid out nude in the sun,
and you glowed white
like a thick, sore thumb.
I could tell you felt uncomfortable
in the brightness,
afraid of what might drop out
of the immense skies
to pluck you away.
The several times
I've taken you skinny-dipping
you've enjoyed — familiar with darkness,
the cool water
gently swaying you back and forth.

Sometimes I wonder
what you would think of this world
if you had eyes and ears
and could walk around,
staring at the birds and trees,
doing routine yard work,
nodding politely to neighbors.
How would you react
to the teenage girls out back
sunning in their bikinis?
What would you say

to the single woman
in the upstairs apartment
who comes over to borrow sugar?
"Hi, my name's David,
but you can call me Dick."
And how would you treat
your own penis,
tucked away between your legs,
aching to break out and in
and in and out,
but so shy
you can hardly ever
get him to make a sound?

The Vision of an Idiot

There's a field with one large tree in the middle, possibly an oak or cedar or maple. No houses for miles in any direction. There's a dog peeing on the tree while watching a newspaper tumble in the wind like a clumsy, albino cat. And the dog thinks: I could catch that cat and eat it. He has his leg up by the tree in a field of young corn. The sky darkens as rain clouds come in from wherever rain clouds come from. The dog is still peeing. By now, the newspaper has galloped out of sight. Suddenly, night arrives with bells on and the picture goes black.

This is the vision that haunts the idiot. Every night, he dreams it. Every day, it appears to him for a few moments and vanishes. He rocks his brain thinking: How long can that dog pee? Where on earth does that newspaper end up? And why have I been chosen to be the keeper of revelations?

The Romantic

"Let us leave pretty women
to men without imagination."
—MARCEL PROUST

You can have
the Monroe's, the Welch's,
Loren's, Robert's, Crawford's.
Help yourself
to all the tanned bathing beauties
in threads of clothing
with silky golden hair,
perfect curves, unbelievable skin.
Everything, to them,
is taken at face value.
That model over there,
mouthing a kiss my way,
actually makes my stomach turn.

I can see right through them.
Beneath the luscious exterior,
              that shell of desire,
lies a dark, empty blackboard
with no chalk, no one left
to write anything
meaningful.

I'm looking for the dumpy one,
clumsy and lonesome,
with sturdy, healthy legs and arms,
someone with the kind of personal substance
looks can't compete with.
Hair disheveled, glasses taped
at the side, one panty hose
hugging her left ankle,
and a button missing
down the back:
that's my type.

I can only imagine
what's underneath
that dress.

My Edson Phase
(with great respect and admiration)

The father says, No, no, no, no.

The son says, Why?

No, I said, says the father.

But...

No, no, no. How many times do I have to say it? No. I mean no. No means no.

The mother from the other room says, Russell? Will you please stop?

No, I said, no, I said no, no, no.

But father, you don't realize how much this means to me, offers the son.

No, you're wrong, again, but when you suddenly turn into a vicious ape and come at me like flies on shit, I will be forced to shoot you, eat you, and deposit you into the city sewer system.

Russell! yells mother. Stop teasing Junior!

The father says, No, dammit. I'm the one in charge here.

You're being unreasonable, says mother.

And since when, the father asks, did it become a crime to be unreasonable?

You're a dummy-head, says mother.

You're a mouse gonad, says father.

You're a poop tart.

You're a mosquito with no wings stuck in a huge bowl of spit.

The son says, No, no, no, no.

The mother and father say, Why?

And so it begins to never end.

View of a Pair

"In some communities in the Himalayas,
to show respect for her husband's guests,
a wife greeted them with her breasts bared."
—*Detroit Free Press*

It's just luck
to get stuck
in the wrong country.
Maybe we could start
a massive letter-writing campaign,
a lobbying group, simulated Himalayan villages
strategically located to help bring
this one tradition to the U.S.
Can you imagine walking
over to your friend's house,
his wife answering the door,
"Oh, hi Betty," you say.
"Kind of nippy tonight, eh?"
Some would droop; some would seem to tip
backwards into the chest; others round and firm,
the exact color of desire.
The nursing mothers would open the door
dripping milk across the landing.
The problem becomes which pair
should you stare at, eyes or breasts?
Or one of each?

I know I don't have to worry
because it will never happen here.
All I can do is sit back and imagine
a woman baring her breasts
for her husband's friends,
the renewed popularity in visiting.
And I am the biggest guest.
I walk down the street and
every door flings open,
women stepping out to greet me,
swaying a little,
all of them, in some way,
utterly beautiful.

Only on Sundays

The whorehouse
is a restored barn
sectioned off into rooms.
On Sundays
they line the men up
against one wall
while the women
stand naked against
the other. The first
man to carry his hat
on his dick
across the room
gets his pick
of the girls.

Sometimes
on quiet Sunday nights
you can stand in town
by the General Store
and hear the women laughing
as they watch these men
drop their pants and
shuffle across the floor:
some falling,
some never starting,
some almost looking
as if they were giving birth
to a midget
wearing a hat.

The Other Side of the Coin

"Intercourse is the pure, sterile, formal expression of men's contempt for women."
—Andrea Dworkin

I hate my wife
when she lets me kiss the curve in her lower back
and move up the spine to the neck, the ear.
And then there's the licking,
tonguing the moist lips
of a vagina—I despise
having to do this night after night.
Or actually entering her
while gently kissing her nipples,
standing up firm in the moonlight,
that's the worst
feeling of all.
It's amazing to think
of the immense sterilization
we've been through
all because deep down inside
I revile her and her kind.
It makes me stop to wonder:
what would we do
to each other
if it weren't for contempt?

Dear Future

You're one step ahead of me
At every turn. The shy, silent type,
You prefer the back booth,
Candle-lit, out of sight
But within striking distance.
For the longest time,
I thought you couldn't speak,
But the past told me you
"choose not to."

Give me one evening, you and me alone,
Over beers, and let's be frank.
Tell me straight to my face.
Will I get the promotion?
The convertible? The cute little bungalow
On the bay? Will I live to kiss my grandchildren's
Children? Will this knee really have to be
Replaced? Will I see 80? Will I go
Before my wife?

But you blend into dusk, the night,
The city, and I'm left to watch shadows
Stretch out under a full moon.
We'll meet, I'm sure,
At least once more
At a time of your choosing.
I'm warning you now:
Be ready to duck.

The Tired of Your Present Life Tree Game

Find some string and tie your hair to a tree. It is least painful when you allow your feet to touch the ground. Stay as close to the trunk as possible. The object of the game is to become the tree.

You must stand silently and still. Close your eyes and go blank, mindless, swaying a little in the wind. Let the sound of rustling leaves occupy your total existence. Try to sleep for long periods. Dream bark. Dream branch. Dream deep, cool wood. When a robin builds a nest on your head or shoulder, untie yourself and start a new life.

The Poet: Number Two
Heard at an introduction to a poetry reading:
"This next poet really knows how to cut the cheese."

        As do all good poets.
It helps to practice
one's sense of timing, delivery,
resonance, rhythm and texture.
        And the best poems
permeate a room, stuck there in mid-air,
smelling of the stuff of life—steamed cabbage,
baked beans, tacos, onion soup, Cajun Dave's chili.
        As with all basic human acts,
there's nothing to be ashamed of
when you say you write poetry.
But there's more to it
than just blowing hot air
and holding onto the seat of your pants.
        There's a rare talent
to letting one rip
and leaving behind
an audience grimacing
with the hard fact
that sometimes life stinks
and you have to endure it.

Voices

He heard voices. They came from the ants he killed, from the yellow pepper, from the parakeet, from the black tarred roof on the shed. One voice was an apple falling to the ground. It said, "Shit, not again." Then it rolled over on its mouth and was silent.

The man told no one about the voices. He was afraid, both of what people would think, and of what would happen to the voices if he spoke about them. Maybe they would stop. To him, they sounded like leaves in the trees, voices like gentle clapping, rising louder and diminishing, like whispers. Once a chair asked him, "Are you comfortable?" A flower said, "Will you water me, please? I'm so thirsty." So he did. He heard the grass humming a song. The sky was yelling, "Hey! Look up here. Come on!"

The man lit a cigar. They talked for at least thirty minutes about the politics of cruelty before he snuffed it out. Even after that, he and the butt discussed how it was that some people died courageously and others were pushed and pulled, clawing their way into the unknown. "Ashes to ashes, as I've always said," said the cigar. That apparently was the last word on the subject since the air around the man stood up and clapped, cheering loudly.

Dear Death

Let's make a deal:
you ignore me
and I'll ignore you.
Hell, there are millions
of other people and animals
and insects out there:
play with them.
I'll forget you even exist.
I'll live each day
without a thought of the end,
without grief,
my whole life without fear.

I know we'll meet
face-to-ugly face eventually,
and you'll have your way with me,
but until then
let me go walking along,
oblivious and stupid.
Let me see the dark clouds coming
and think it's going to rain.
Let me hear bells tolling
and remember the sweet music.
Let me smell the decay
and imagine good, rich compost.
And let me stare at the writing
on the wall
and say
it's poetry
it's beautiful
I wish I had written that.

The Meaning of Life
"Define yourself or be defined."
—highway graffiti

I don't know
who the hell I am
so tell me, please.
I need someone
to define this crazy world
and me in it.
And don't be polite.
I can handle
idiot, asshole, shithead.
I read once that everyone's
an absolute fool
for five minutes each day
and that wisdom comes
in not exceeding the limit.
But I have no limits,
or at least I don't know
where they are.
Tell me the meaning
of this job, these kids,
this woman I sleep with and love,
these poems that hang on my heels
like mud, like dogshit,
like candy wrappers
that won't come loose.
I wake up in the morning
and take up the world,
letting it all in
but I can't honestly say
I'm any better, or worse,
or different.
I'm just me,
a guy driving to work,
a guy mowing the lawn,
a guy walking his children
to the ice cream shop,
hoping to God
they're not out
of marble fudge.

Instructions for My Funeral
for Nick Bozanic

Nobody can wear black,
except me.
I want to be dressed in a tuxedo,
bow tie, patent leather shoes,
an all black wrist watch,
           stopped.
I want beer, wine, soda,
coffee and tea available,
free of charge, accompanied
by several cheese and vegetable trays,
barbeque chips, pretzels, Hershey kisses.

The eulogy should be full of the bad jokes
I was known for,
several poems read, and a word of praise
for the natural order, of which
I am merely a part.
After a brief ceremony,
no one is allowed to follow me
to the graveyard.

I want everyone to drive to the hall
for dinner, drinks, a live band and dancing.
Outside, volleyball and horseshoes.
At a table, my latest book should be sold
at half-price. I've pre-signed fifty copies
in the closet for the occasion.
No contribution to anything or anyone
is requested.
No grieving or crying will be tolerated.
Life is too important
to be bothered with despair of any kind.
I want noise. Music. Laughter.

The slapping of backs. Jokes.
Hugs. Stories. I want smiles
on the faces of my children and relatives,
on my wife and good friends.
I want people touching each other.
In this small moment of silence
I want anything but silence.
I'll get enough of that where I'm going.
And so will all of you.

How Do You Spell Relief?
"God loves a clean urinal."

He despises cigarette butts,
moldy gum, toilet paper, half-chewed cigars,
candy wrappers and pubic hair
jostling in the rush
of a flush.
He deplores brown water stains
etching down the urinal wall
like muted varicose veins.
The little blue chunks
of deodorant circling the drain
make him gag.

In heaven,
the urinals sparkle in a crystal light.
Not a speck. Not a mark.
Never a drip of urine
spotting the wall or floor.
Never a puddle to stand in.
God loves to step into the men's room,
open his royal robe,
and let it flow,
convinced
He has the world
in the palm of his hand.

The Pretend You're Not Alive Game

The theory is you have to die someday, so you might as well practice. Dying is not like getting a haircut; it's permanent. When your name is called, you want to get it right.

First, force yourself to sleep for longer and longer periods. Work on this until you can sleep for 24 hours straight. Practice blocking out voices, alarms, music, birds, trains. Mark your position in bed and lie still until when you wake up the next day you are in the exact same position. Now you are ready for step two.

You can do it anywhere but a crowded street or office or store is usually ideal. Practice collapsing, letting your legs go out, body crumbling in a heap. When people touch you, shake your shoulder, ask if you're all right, don't move or talk. Practice not breathing for two minute intervals. You're making progress when you begin taking ambulance rides.

The first one to hear a bystander say, "I think he's dead," is the winner. Stand up quickly, brushing off your arms and legs, and walk away from everyone, unsmiling, deadpan. Real death will be a cinch.

One Night Stand

I slept with death
last night.
I'm not proud of it.
Yes, there was sex and sweat
as we both tried to disappear

into instinct, but it wasn't right.
Like two broken mannequins,
we banged into each other,
flailing out of spite.
And then she slept, and snored, the bitch.

The Moo Game

Take off your shoes and socks and place your feet in a pail of milk (if you prefer, you may warm the milk). While mooing, imagine the wall in front of you to be a hill, with grass, with a stream and butterflies. Moo and moo until the sound of your own voice vibrates through your spinal cord.

Then put a sock over your head and sing the milk song, making up verses as you go: Milk is my friend, we drink all the time, white as a snowflake, or anything that rhymes. After the song, stand up straight and suck hard, pretending to be a straw.

To end the game, step out of the pail and pour the milk on your calves. Watch what they do to it.

The Season for Leaving

It was spring and the woman, a faithful wife and mother whose children had grown and moved away, decided to become a mermaid. She fastened flippers to her feet instead of shoes, practiced walking through the house. Hours upon hours, she spent in the bathtub, submerging herself for 2, 3, 4 minutes at a time. For months, she prepared in the privacy of her home.

"I've decided to become a mermaid," she confessed to her husband. He shrugged his shoulders.

"Was it something I did, or didn't do?"

"No, you're fine. It's just what I've always wanted. And what better time than now?"

"Does this mean I have to make my own dinner?"

"Yes," she said. "For the rest of your life." And she flopped out of the house, down Loomis Street, to the shoreline. She wasn't sure there were mermaids in Lake Michigan, but she'd find out or be the first.

A curious crowd gathered around her. She undressed, waded out into the cold water, and started swimming straight away from the people on shore who were now clapping, shouting encouragement to her. As she dove underwater, kicking deeper and deeper, she heard faint singing floating up from the bottom, saw faces in the shadows. Sisters, she thought, and opened her mouth, lungs, to become one of them.

Back home, the husband fried a hot dog in a pan and said, "Damn mermaids."

The Substitute

The teacher slumped forward, banging his forehead on the desk. The students were silent, staring, until Patsy Lou, from her front row seat, threw a pencil and hit the teacher, thwack, on his bald spot. Nothing. The drug sprinkled into Mr. Stidham's coffee had worked, just as Tommy said it would.

Within minutes, the boys had carried the teacher to the table, and the girls were gloved, wearing face masks. Mary made the first cut from the throat to the navel. Lynn clipped the main arteries and held the heart up to applause. The rest of them took turns cutting, dissecting, finding organs and naming them with incredible accuracy. Molloy tied an artery around his neck like a set of pearls. Little Kate was collecting toes and fingers. Rodriquez grabbed the saw and was just starting brain surgery when the principal walked in.

"Jesus Christ," he said. "This is the third sub this week."

"Well, you know, this is biology class," Elizabeth said.

"I realize that, but, dammit!" He stormed out and slammed the door.

Rodriquez started sawing again. "Wait til you guys see the hypothalamus. And the pons. Man, this stuff is so cool."

God Takes Up Golf

More of a walker,
He rarely uses a cart.
The golf bag floats in mid-air
following behind Him, the right club
easing out and into His hands at will.
God's swing is picture perfect,
though He sometimes tries
to put more into it than necessary.
Only a few will give Him advice—
Moses, David, Abraham.
They know He doesn't need it,
but it helps to pass the time.
A small spectator crowd of angels,
archangels, and cherubims trail within earshot,
singing hymns of green praise.

God can't help but think of the front nine
as the Old Testament, through narrow woods
and deep valleys, the back nine
as the New Testament, wide open and forgiving.
The prophets and apostles humor the almighty
as they lay down bet after bet, playing God one-on-one.
They never win. They may take a skin
every century or so, but it's rare.
Only Christ can give the old man
a run for His money.
It usually ends up in a shoot-out after eighteen,
sudden death,
and you know
how that goes.

The Plain Truth

"A man thinks in a straight line.
A woman thinks in circles."
— Harriet Fields

1.
I always knew there was a difference
but could never think my way
around it.
Thank you, Harriet,
for putting it straight to me.

2.
Thinking strictly linear,
it follows then that bisexuals think
in semi-circles,
homosexuals
in squiggles and doodles.
With sex change operations,
advanced geometry
becomes an issue.

3.
All men think the same
as they wait in line
for the presidency,
in line for a raise,
for milk or beer,
for an unemployment check,
in line for the urinal.

4.
Women huddle together
around the table,
thoughts whirling through their brains.
There is no urgency in their voices;
if they forget to say something,

they know it will come back to them,
as usual, in time.

5.
Of course, we pay the price
for such simplicity.
A man climbing straight up
the company ladder, making money,
working late,
falls over dead on his square desk.
His friends line up to see him at the funeral.
A woman swallows little round valiums
and shakes her head.
No matter how far she drives,
she goes nowhere, returning to the same house
and screaming kids and ugly husband,
the lines on his face making motions
she will never understand.

6.
It must be nice to be Harriet Fields,
to know the secrets of human nature,
of life itself, to draw such definite conclusions.
Meanwhile, the rest of us go on living
in our ignorance trying to intersect,
to make a smudge here or there,
to connect with someone,
knowing only the truth:
a line never ends,
a circle never begins.

Last Thing a Man Would Ever Say
"Sometimes, I just want to be held."
—SCOTT EPSTEIN

It could happen.
Most of us guys, deep down,
way, way down, like down a blackhole
burrowing into their bodies, somewhere
toward the core, somewhere
out of sight and sound,
have a tender side, a side that blushes
and wants to cuddle up with extra blankets,
a sappy romance novel,
and just the touch of a woman's
smooth leg against leg,
thigh on thigh.
On some level, we all want to be held,
and not where you're thinking,
but held like a good friend or cousin
or the way a mother wraps
herself around her infant,
with humming and quiet words
and the vague chance
of a brand new life.

How to Fall in Love with Country Music

it creeps into your life
like fungus
like cold sores
like your old high school girlfriend
suddenly appearing
at the doorstep
missing half of her teeth
and claiming to be the mother
of two of your children

it simply wears on you
the twang of the steel guitar
grating against your better judgment
always the sad voice recreating
a life of divorcees and pick-up trucks
and bar fights and driving the lone road
to Omaha
and the more you listen
the easier it is to believe
your mother really did run off with the mailman
and you were fired for pissing on the boss' desk
and the woman you love
loves your best friend's
dad

you don't fall in love with country music
it falls in love with you or rather
it breaks down one small section of the brain
and you become helpless
to the urge to wear a cowboy hat
to learn the Texas two-step
to buy a gunrack
and all along
the music is telling you
just how lonely you are
and damn
                      if it's not true

A Burning Bush of Sorts

God spoke to me while I sat alone on the park bench. It was a sunny day, early spring; I could see buds on the trees.

"So, what do you think?" He said.

"About what?"

"All this life busting out around you."

I didn't expect God to say "busting out." I expected manifesting or conjuring.

"It's wonderful," I said. "Nice work."

"Do you think there are too many birds? I could cut back on a few species."

"No, not at all. It's the return of the birds that makes me think of spring."

For me, the return of the robin was the beginning of spring. My wife says the first robin around our house is her grandmother, checking in on us. She used to love seeing the first robin. Then, the idea struck me.

"Here's a question for you, God. Is that first robin we see every year our Grandma Ketterer?"

"Oh, I don't know. I'd have to check the inventory and that takes awhile up here."

"But in theory," I said, "do the dead come back to visit us as animals? Or as living things, in general?"

"It's possible," He said. "With me, anything is possible, you know."

I took that as a yes, thanked him, and ran home to tell my wife the good news.

Return of the Grim Reaper
(after Charles Simic)

I hadn't seen him since grandpa died,
but he looked good.
"Atkins diet," he admitted. "Lost 25 pounds
since the new year. Look how loose
this robe is on me."
It was true: his dark robe in tatters
blew around him in a storm with lightning
flashing only within the robe itself.
I could see his stick-like calves.

He wanted to know where my parents
were this winter.
"Snow birds," I said. "The Alabama coast."
"Yeah, I've been meaning to drop by,
but I've been so busy
with all this terrorist crap going on.
No rest for the weary."
He laughed at that last line, but ended up
hacking, bending over, coughing up blood
which was sucked back into the robe
by the storm.

After he left,
I realized I should have lied about my parents,
said Nevada or Phoenix, the Florida Keys.
There is so much,
now that I think about it,
that I should have done.

I'll Take Your Face

I'll take your face
& plaster it on every skyscraper,
bank, school, chimney,
every door, window, wall, fish tank.
You are the one and only for me,
the cat's meow, the key that fits,
the fuel that fires my major league motor.
You can swing me like a poodle.
You can flip me like a bird.
You can squeeze me into lemonade
with one quirky smile.
I can talk about poetry,
I can show you how to hit a backhand,
I can make a mean bowl of chili,
but I can't explain love.
If you ripped open my chest & grabbed my heart,
you'd find the answer somewhere at the core.

Until then, I'll take your eyes to memorize.
I'll take your hips to live in.
I'll take your hands for worship.
I'll take your legs to eat.
& I'll take your wet lips
& pray they plant themselves on my body,
take root & blossom
over every inch of flesh,
petals blooming everywhere
until I'm beautiful enough
for you.